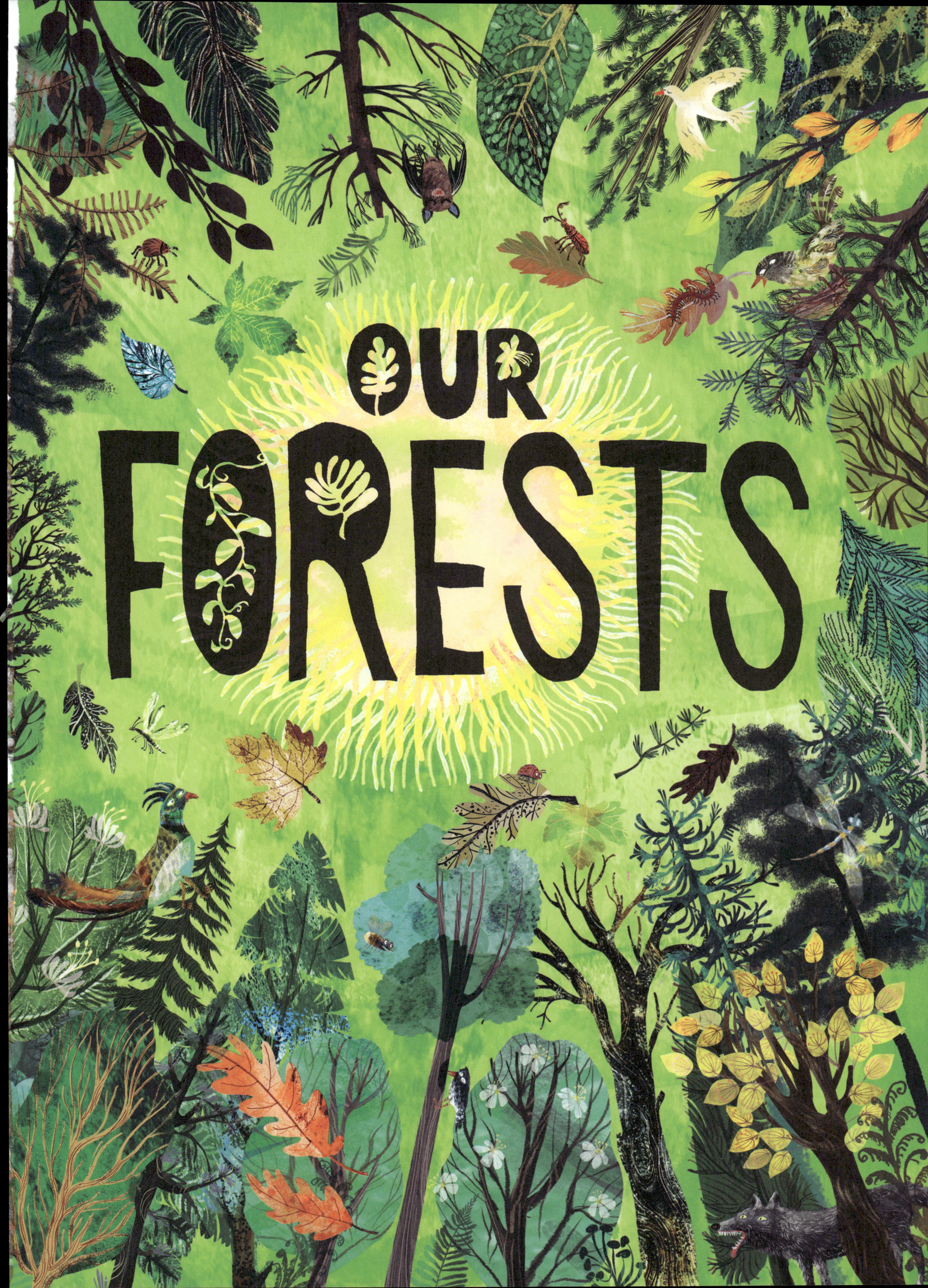
OUR
FORESTS

Words and pictures

YUVAL ZOMMER

**Can you find...**

...9 golden acorns hidden in this book?

OUR
FORESTS
t&h

# CONTENTS

# WHAT IS A FOREST?

Forests are large spaces packed with trees and wildlife. Nearly a third of our planet's land is covered by them. It can take hundreds of years for a forest to fully grow.

### Forest edge

The edge of a forest gets more sunlight than the deep, dark centre. The extra light allows more plants to grow here.

### Grassy glades

A glade is an open area amongst the trees. You might find deer munching the grass here.

## Forest maze

Some forests have paths between the trees, which make them easy to explore. But sometimes thick bushes, tangled vines and fallen trees can block the way.

## Wood wide web

Underground, a complicated web of roots, fungi and bacteria connect all the trees together.

# TROPICAL RAINFOREST

## Does it always rain in a rainforest?

Not everyday, but it's always wet and steamy. Amazon rainforests are criss-crossed with lakes, streams and rivers. During the rainy season, the areas near rivers are flooded for half the year.

### Walking tree

This palm tree can 'walk' to a sunnier spot on its stilt-like roots by killing off roots on the shady side and growing new ones in the sun.

### Spot the spots

The jaguar is the top hunter here. Its spotty coat blends in with the sun-dappled jungle to help it creep up on its prey.

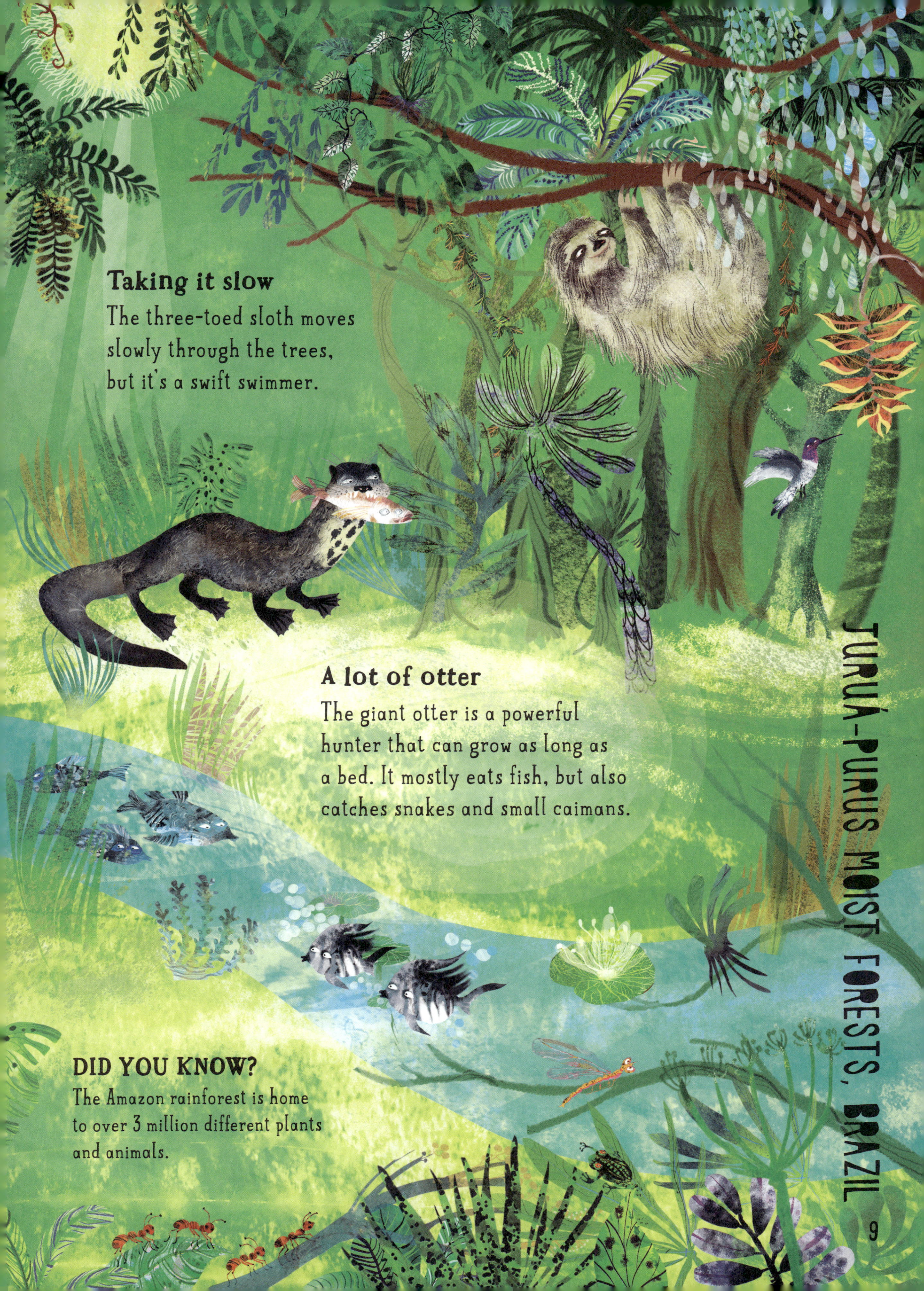

# JURUÁ-PURUS MOIST FORESTS, BRAZIL

**Taking it slow**

The three-toed sloth moves slowly through the trees, but it's a swift swimmer.

**A lot of otter**

The giant otter is a powerful hunter that can grow as long as a bed. It mostly eats fish, but also catches snakes and small caimans.

**DID YOU KNOW?**

The Amazon rainforest is home to over 3 million different plants and animals.

# BLACK FOREST

**Forests are green, so why is this one black?**

From afar, the dark green trees in this forest look almost black. They grow so close together that very little light can get into the dark and mysterious forest!

**Fairy tale forest**

This magical forest inspired the Grimm brothers to write their famous tales, including *Snow White* and *Sleeping Beauty*.

**Nosey pig**

Wild boar root around on the forest floor. Their super snouts can sniff out acorns, shoots, worms and insects buried underground.

## Wandering wolves

Humans hunted wolves in the Black Forest until there were none left. But now, 150 years later, they're back! They travelled here themselves from Poland.

### DID YOU KNOW?

You can tell the different evergreen trees apart, because fully grown fir cones point upwards and pine and spruce cones hang down.

## Deadly or delicious?

Hundreds, if not thousands, of different fungi grow in this forest, including some edible mushrooms. But beware! Some are deadly poisonous.

# THE BLACK FOREST, GERMANY

# TYPES OF FOREST

## Are forests all the same?

No! Different types of forests grow in different parts of the world.

### Boreal forests

Boreal forests are found in the freezing north. Most trees that grow there are conifers such as pine, spruce and fir, which have needles instead of leaves.

### Urban forests

All the trees that grow within a town or city count as a forest, too! They help keep the air in our cities clean and provide homes for wildlife.

## Temperate forests

These forests change with the seasons – they're warm in summer and chilly in winter. They contain lots of deciduous trees, which drop their leaves in autumn and regrow them in the spring.

## Tropical forests

Tropical forests grow in places where it is hot all year round. Many tropical forests are rainforests, which get a lot of rain. They are lush, leafy and packed full of wildlife.

# CLOUD FOREST

BWINDI IMPENETRABLE FOREST, UGANDA

## Can trees catch clouds?

They can in a cloud forest! As well as using their roots to soak up water, the trees here capture water through their leaves, as mist and clouds drift by.

## Sky garden

The forest is full of epiphytes – plants that use other plants for support. Mosses cover tree bark, and ferns and orchids grow on branches.

## Tangled trees

Strolling through this 'impenetrable' forest is tricky. The trees here are tangled together, with crooked, twisted trunks.

## Hard to swallow

The African giant swallowtail is the biggest butterfly in Africa. Its wings stretch as wide as a dinner plate and it is poisonous to predators who try to eat it.

## DID YOU KNOW?

At night, small gorillas nest in trees, making beds out of bent branches. Heavier gorillas sleep in grassy nests on the ground.

## Super troop

Over 400 mountain gorillas live here in large family groups, called troops. Their thick fur keeps them warm near the cold mountaintops.

# EUCALYPTUS FOREST

## Can these trees ease a sneeze?

The leaves of eucalyptus trees are full of scented oil, which can help clear a stuffy nose. Eucalyptus is also used in insect repellents and creams for soothing aches and pains.

### Tree huggers

Eucalyptus leaves are poisonous to most animals, but koalas have a special organ to digest them.

### Bats not bees

Flying foxes are giant bats that feed on fruit and nectar at night. Like bees, they pollinate the plants they visit, including eucalyptus and fig trees.

## BONGIL BONGIL NATIONAL PARK, AUSTRALIA

**Cockatoo calls**

The loud cries of cockatoos echo through the forest. These birds eat the seeds of eucalyptus trees.

**Burning up**

Climate change is threatening Australia's wildlife. In 2019 deadly wildfires swept through the country's forests, killing nearly three billion animals, including koalas.

# FOREST PROTECTORS

## Who lives in forests?

About 300 million people live in the world's forests. Among them are Indigenous communities who have been living in harmony with their forests for many generations, passing down knowledge of how to care for them.

### Living with tigers

The Soliga people from South India have peacefully lived alongside tigers for centuries. By caring for and guarding the forest, these people are helping to protect these endangered big cats.

### Honey haven

Locals of Gura Ferda forest in Ethiopia hang bee hives in the trees. The honey they collect helps them make money and the trees are protected from being cut down.

### Reindeer herders

Many Sámi people from the chilly far north of Scandinavia and Russia are fighting to protect the boreal forests where they have herded reindeer for centuries.

### Fighting fire with fire

Native Americans have a tradition called 'cultural burning' where they light small, controlled fires to keep forests healthy. These little fires can help reduce the risk of big wildfires.

# BOREAL FOREST

## Why is it dark in the daytime?

Boreal forests grow at the top of the world. Hossa is so far north that in summer the sun never sets, and in mid-winter the sun does not rise. In January there is hardly any daylight!

## Lighting up the night

This dark forest is a good place to see the northern lights, where colourful swirls dance across the night sky.

## Freezing forest

Thick snow covers the ground from December to April and the temperature can drop to -30°C. Even in summer, there is layer of frozen ground beneath the surface called permafrost.

# HOSSA NATIONAL PARK, FINLAND

**Ghostly owl**

The great grey owl is the largest owl in the world. It is known as the 'ghost of the forest' because it flies silently and is hard to spot.

**Snow gear**

Reindeer have thick fur to keep them warm. Their splayed hooves stop them sinking into the snow, like snowshoes, and have sharp edges that grip the ice.

# FROM ROOTS TO CANOPY

## Why do rainforests have layers?

The closely packed trees in a rainforest form 4 layers, or storeys, like a block of flats. Each layer has particular conditions that suit the animals and plants that live in it.

### The emergent layer

Here, trees as tall as 20-storey buildings sway in the wind and soak up sunshine. Birds of prey, bats, butterflies and some monkeys live up here.

### The canopy

This thick, leafy layer of treetops is like the forest's roof. Fruit and nuts grow here, attracting insects, birds and monkeys.

## The understorey

Below the canopy it's shady, sheltered and damp – perfect for frogs and snakes. Plants have larger leaves to soak up any available sunlight and vines wrap around trees.

## The forest floor

It is dark and damp and the ground is covered in a blanket of dead leaves. Many larger animals such as elephants and big cats live here.

# PRIMEVAL FOREST

## Can forests show us the past?

This is a protected primeval forest, which means it's very old and has barely been touched by humans. It looks the same as it did thousands of years ago.

### Meet the emperors

Lots of different trees grow here, but tall old oaks reign over the forest, with grand names like Dominator Oak and Emperor of the North.

### Rotten homes

Broken branches, rotting stumps and fallen trees are everywhere. Rotting wood creates safe homes for lots of wildlife, including bats, bugs and beetles.

# BIAŁOWIEŻA FOREST, POLAND AND BELARUS

**Welcome back**

Herds of European bison roam wild. In the past, they were hunted until the only ones left lived in zoos. In the 1950s a few were returned to the park and now there are over 900.

**Fungus frenzy**

Many mushrooms and other fungi grow on dead wood. This forest is full of at least 4,000 different types.

# MANGROVE FOREST

## Why is this forest flooded?

Mangrove forests are flooded by salty seawater twice a day as the tide rises and falls along warm coastlines. The freshwater from rivers and streams mixes with salty seawater in these forests.

## Cool cat

Over 200 Bengal tigers live in the forest. These water-loving cats cool off in streams and swim across wide rivers to reach fresh hunting grounds.

## Hidden danger

Saltwater crocodiles are the world's largest living reptile. They lurk in the water, waiting for passing fish, turtles, monkeys or other animals to snatch in their strong jaws.

### Just stopping by

Mangrove forests make great places for migrating birds to rest on their long journeys. 139 different birds come here every year and many stay all winter.

### Super roots

Mangrove trees have special roots that filter out the salt in the seawater. The tall roots are like stilts, holding the tree trunks above the rising tide.

### Safe haven

Beneath the water, the tangled roots of mangroves form a cage where small fish and sea creatures can hide from hungry predators.

## SUNDARBANS, INDIA AND BANGLADESH

# FOREST FAIRY TALES

## Do you want to hear a story?

The forests of the world hold many stories of mystical beings. Some are spooky spirits, others are tricky tricksters and many are protectors of the forest.

### Connected for life

In ancient Greece, hamadryads were female nature spirits and forest protectors whose lives were each tied to an individual tree. If a hamadryad's tree died, so would they.

### Russian rascal

In Russian folk tales, the Leshy is a mischievous spirit as tall and leafy as the trees he protects. He plays pranks on travellers and can be heard laughing, or whistling through the trees.

### Walking backwards

In the Amazon rainforest, there are stories of a sneaky boy called the Curupira. He has feet that point backwards, so anyone who follows his tracks will be led the wrong way.

### Forest friends

The kodama are wispy tree spirits from Japan's most ancient forests. Cutting down a kodama's tree can bring terrible misfortune, but protecting trees brings good luck.

### Little woodsman

In Gotland, Sweden, Bysen is a gnome-like creature who roams the forests, carrying an axe. He enchants people and makes them lose their way.

# ANCIENT WOODLAND

## Why is this forest historic?

Sherwood Forest is very old! Trees have grown here for 10,000 years. If they could talk, they'd tell you stories of kings, queens and famous thieves.

### Majorly old

The Major Oak is the oldest tree in the forest. It sprouted from an acorn about 1,000 years ago and has outlived over 50 kings and queens since!

### Forest of kings

William the Conqueror made Sherwood a royal hunting forest – which meant only the king and his friends were allowed to hunt deer here.

# SHERWOOD FOREST, UK

## Robber Robin

According to legend, the famous outlaw Robin Hood lived here with his band of merry men. He robbed the rich and gave money to the poor.

## Spooky 'shrooms

Some creepy fungi grow here! Sticky beefsteak fungus looks like raw, bloody meat. Dead man's fingers look like a buried hand reaching out of the ground to grab you!

# REDWOOD FOREST

REDWOOD NATIONAL PARK, USA

## Are there giants in the forest?

Redwoods are the biggest trees on Earth. They tower above you like giants. Fossils have been found of ancient redwoods that grew 200 million years ago, when dinosaurs walked the Earth.

### A very big secret

Hyperion is the world's tallest known living tree. It measures 116 metres – as high as a 30-storey skyscraper! It grows in this forest but its exact location is kept secret to protect it.

### Skydiving squirrels

Flying squirrels glide from tree to tree on skin stretched between their arms and legs. Their bushy tails are used to steer and slow down as they come in to land.

## Rooting for each other

Redwoods twist their roots together with their neighbours' to share nutrients and stop them from toppling over in strong winds.

## Clambering canines

Grey foxes are one of the only canines that can climb trees. They use their strong, sharp, curved claws to grip tree trunks.

# FORESTS FOR THE FUTURE

## How do forests help our planet?

Forests are not just an important source of food and shelter for people and wildlife, they are vital for the health of our planet. When forests are cut down, we lose much more than just trees.

### Breathe in

Forests are Earth's big, leafy lungs. Trees and plants release oxygen, the gas that people and animals need to breathe to stay alive.

### Happy homes

Forests are home to about 8 out of 10 of all living things that are found on land.

## Cool down

Forests can slow down the effects of climate change. Trees absorb carbon dioxide, which is the gas that traps heat in the Earth's atmosphere and causes global warming.

## Drink up

Forests help to prevent flooding because the roots of large trees suck up hundreds of litres of water.

# TEMPERATE RAINFOREST

## What's the temperature in a rainforest?

Not all rainforests are hot and steamy. These rare temperate rainforests grow in places that are rainy and mild. Moisture-loving moss and lichen covers everything.

### An ancient story

First Nations people have lived in the rainforest for over 10,000 years. One of their legends tells that spirit bears were created as a reminder of the last Ice Age, when Earth was covered in huge sheets of ice.

### Sleepy heads

Bears sleep through most of the winter. They doze in a den for four or five months without eating, drinking, peeing or pooing. They wake up ravenous in spring.

# GREAT BEAR RAINFOREST, CANADA

## Room to roost

Bald eagles build enormous nests high up in ancient trees. The nests can weigh as much as a walrus.

## Rare bear

This forest got its name because it's full of bears – including grizzlies and black bears. If you're lucky you might spy a rare, creamy-coloured spirit bear.

# BAMBOO FOREST

## Is bamboo a skinny tree?

Although it can grow as tall as a tree, bamboo is actually a type of grass with woody stems. It grows underneath other forest trees on the mountain slopes of southwest China.

### Picky eaters

The only giant pandas left in the wild live in these forests. They eat bamboo, which isn't very nutritious, so they need to chew through up to 40 kg of it each day.

## Nimble nibblers

Golden takins are goat-like animals. Their split hooves spread out to help them grip the steep, rocky slopes.

## Mountain monkeys

Golden snub-nosed monkeys are known for their bright fur and blue faces. They grow thick coats in winter and huddle together to keep warm.

# MINSHAN AND QINLING MOUNTAINS, CHINA

### DID YOU KNOW?

Bamboos are the fastest growing woody plants in the world. Some can grow up to a metre in 24 hours. That's as tall as a four-year-old!

# FOREST ADVENTURES

## What can I do in the woods?

If you go down to the woods today...there's so much you can do! Don't forget to take an adult along too.

### Listen to the forest

What noises can you hear? Are there any birds singing, trees creaking, twigs snapping or leaves rustling?

### Build a den

Prop long branches and sticks into the fork of a tree to make a cone-shaped frame. Fill in the gaps with extra sticks and leaves, leaving a gap for the entrance.

## Hug a tree

Wrap your arms around a tree and give it a big squeeze! What does it feel like? Is the bark rough or smooth?

## Which way is north?

Look at the trees! More moss will grow on the side of the tree that gets the least sunlight and stays damper – that's north if you live in the northern hemisphere and south in the southern hemisphere.

# WHERE IN THE WORLD?

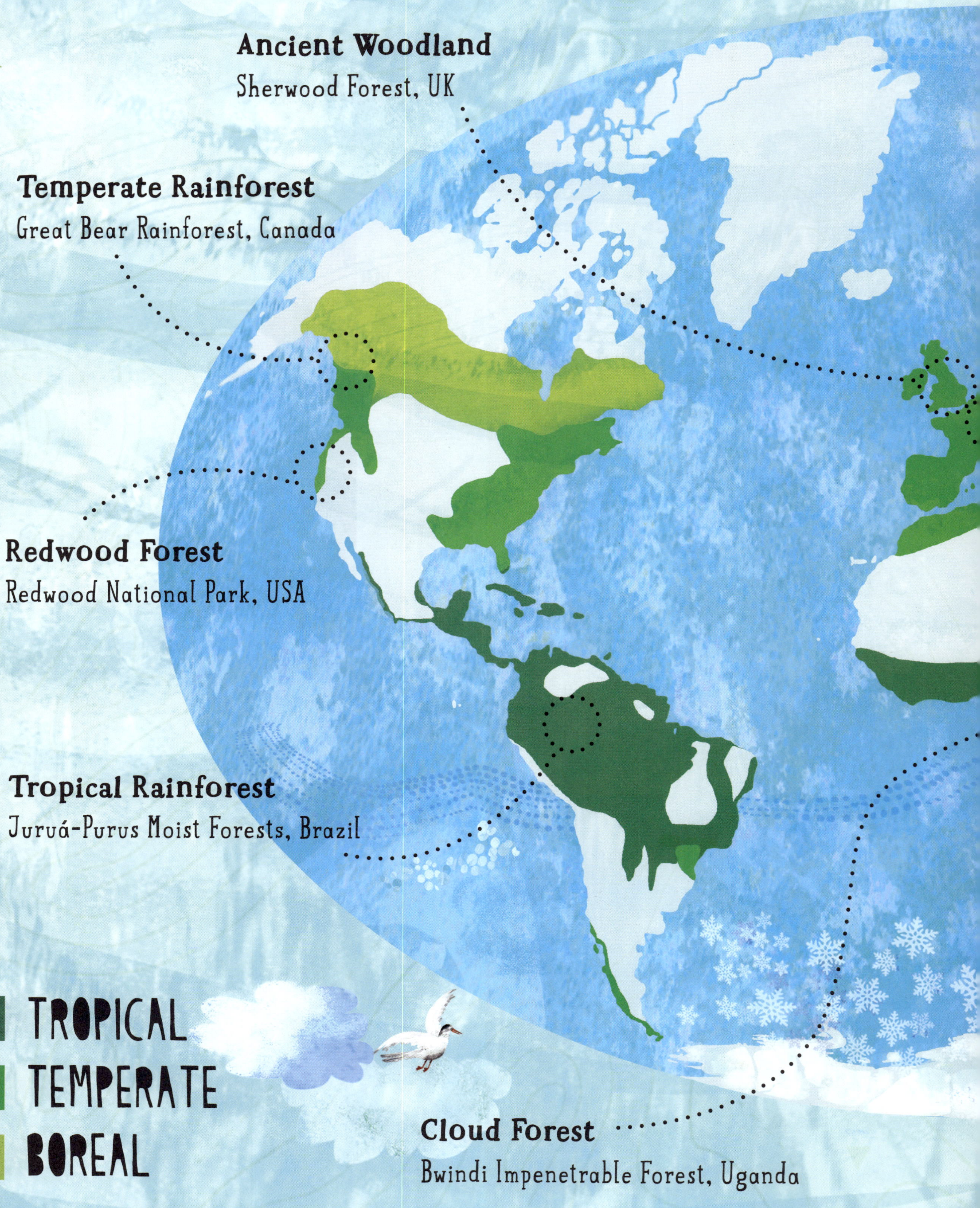

Boreal Forest
Hossa National Park, Finland
Primeval Forest
Białowieża Forest, Poland and Belarus
Black forest
The Black Forest, Germany
Bamboo Forest
Minshan and Qinling Mountains, China
Eucalyptus Forest
Bongil Bongil National Park, Australia
Mangrove Forest
Sundarbans, India and Bangladesh

# DID YOU FIND...

...the 9 golden acorns hidden in the forests?
Did you know that squirrels bury acorns in the ground so they can dig them up again when they get hungry in winter? Millions of these acorns grow into trees every year because the squirrels forget where they hid them!

8–9 Tropical Rainforest

10–11 Black Forest

16–17 Eucayptus Forest

20–21 Boreal Forest

24–25 Primeval Forest

26–27 Mangrove Forest

30–31 Ancient Woodland

36–37 Temperate Rainforest

38–39 Bamboo Forest

# FOREST WORDS

**Canopy**
The top layer of branches and leaves that spread out to form a type of roof in a forest.

**Conifers**
Evergreen trees that produce cones, such as pine, spruce and fir trees.

**Deciduous trees**
Trees that lose their leaves in autumn and winter and grow new ones in spring.

**Evergreen trees**
Trees that stay green and have leaves all year round.

**Ice Age**
A time in the past when temperatures were very cold and large parts of Earth were covered in ice.

**Impenetrable**
Impossible to see or move through.

**Indigenous community**
A group of people who are descendants (relatives) of the first people to live in the country or region where they come from. Indigenous communities from Canada are known as First Nations.

**Rainforest**
Forests where it rains a lot all year round. Rainforests usually contain lots of different plants and animals. Tropical rainforests are found in hot parts of the world and temperate rainforests are found in cooler places.

**Rainy season**
A time of year when a place gets most of its rain. Many tropical countries near the equator (the invisible line around the middle of the Earth) experience really heavy rain and storms for several months of the year.

**Wildfires**
Unplanned and uncontrollable fires that burn in natural environments, such as forests and grasslands. They can be very destructive to wildlife.

# INDEX

To my great-nephew Guri, with love.

First published in the United Kingdom in 2026 by Thames and Hudson Ltd,
6–24 Britannia Street, London WC1X 9JD


Consultancy by Barbara Taylor



EU Authorized Representative: Interart S.A.R.L.
19 rue Charles Auray, 93500 Pantin, Paris, France
productsafety@thameshudson.co.uk
www.interart.fr

A CIP catalogue record for this book is available from the British Library

ISBN 978-0-500-65369-2
01

Printed and bound in China
by Toppan Leefung Printing Ltd.

MIX
Paper | Supporting responsible forestry
FSC® C104723